Contents

KNOCK-KNOCK ROCKS!

JOKE-

TIONARY

JOKES

Tommy NELSON®

An Imprint of Thomas Nelson

JOKE-tionary Jokes
© 2019 by Thomas Nelson

Published in Nashville, Tennessee, by Tommy Nelson. Tommy Nelson
is an imprint of Thomas Nelson. Thomas Nelson is a registered
trademark of HarperCollins Christian Publishing, Inc.

Tommy Nelson titles may be purchased in bulk for educational,
business, fund-raising, or sales promotional use. For information,
please e-mail SpecialMarkets@ThomasNelson.com.

Jokes provided by Tommy Marshall.

ISBN-13: 978-1-4002-1437-2

Printed in the United States of America

19 20 21 22 LSC 6 5 4 3 2 1

Mfr: LSC / Crawfordsville, IN / July 2019 / PO #9541181

Jokes, Jokes, and More Jokes

Q: What do you call it when dinosaurs play bumper cars?

A: Tyrannosaurus wrecks.

Q: How do you know when the moon is going to skip dessert?

A: When it is full.

Q: How do you learn to be a carpenter?

A: You go to boarding school.

Q: How do you make cool music?

A: Put a radio in the fridge.

Q: How do you make fun of a pony that has a sore throat?

A: Say it's a little hoarse.

Q: How do you make fun of a retired vegetable?

A: Call her a has-BEAN.

Q: What did the snorkeler do with the blue whale?

A: Told it some *Knock-Knock Rocks* jokes to try and cheer him up!

Q: What do you call a bear that has lost all its teeth?

A: A gummy bear.

Q: What do you call a cat shaped like a stop sign?

A: An octa-PUSS.

Q: What do you call a cow eating the grass?

A: A lawn MOO-er.

3

Q: What do you call a dinosaur that uses a lot of big words?

A: A TheSAURUS.

Q: What do you call a dog in a garden?

A: A collie-flower.

Q: What do you call a dog on a porch swing?

A: A rocker spaniel.

Q: What do you call a huge mess caused by your kitten?

A: A CATastrophe.

Q: What do you call a lazy baby kangaroo?

A: A pouch potato.

A snail got mugged by a turtle.

Really? What happened?

Nobody knows. When the cops interviewed the snail, it said it all happened too fast!

Two goats ate a DVD and a book.

Really? What happened?

They said they liked the movie, but the book was better.

Q: What do you call a muddy chicken that crosses the road and then comes back?

A: A dirty double-crosser.

Q: What do you call a rhyming lizard?

A: A RAP-tile

Q: What do you call a surgeon with eight arms?

A: A DOC-topus.

Q: What do you call a zebra at the North Pole?

A: Lost.

Q: What do you call fake pasta?

A: MOCK-aroni.

Q: What do you do when your dog has a fever?

A: Cover it in mustard. Nothing is better for a hot dog!

Q: What do you get from a belly-dancing cow?

A: A milkshake.

Q: What do you get when you combine a bird, a dog, and a car?

A: A flying car-pet.

Q: What do you get when you cross a caterpillar and a parrot?

A: A walkie-talkie.

Q: What do you get when you cross a German shepherd with a giraffe?

A: A watchdog for your tree fort.

Q: What do you do if your pet mouse won't stop squeaking?

A: Oil it.

Q: What do you get when you cross a star and a marksman?

A: A shooting star.

Q: What do you get when you cross a T. Rex with a pig?

A: Jurassic pork.

Q: What do you get when you divide the circumference of a pumpkin by its diameter?

A: Pumpkin Pi.

What did one strawberry say to the other?

I don't know. What?

If you hadn't been so fresh, we probably wouldn't be in this jam!

· ·

How do we know God trusts medicine?

I don't know. How?

He gave Moses two tablets.

Q: What insect loves music?

A: A HUM-bug.

Q: What is a blind dinosaur called?

A: An I-don't-think-he-saurus.

Q: What is the name of the man rolling in the leaves?

A: Russell.

Q: What is white and fluffy and swings from cake to cake?

A: A MERINGUE-utan.

Q: What kind of crackers do firemen put in their soup?

A: Firecrackers!

Q: What kind of bull is always sleeping?

A: A bull-dozer.

Q: What is worse than a kitten in a tree?

A: Two kittens in a tree.

Q: When do you go at red and stop at green?

A: When you're eating a watermelon.

Q: When is a sponge really tired?

A: When it is wiped.

Q: Where do you catch the Egyptian flu?

A: From your mummy.

Q: Where was Abraham's temple?

A: On the side of Abraham's head.

Q: Which dog always wins races?

A: The weiner.

Q: Why did the cat eat a lemon?

A: It was a sour puss.

Q: Why did the judge bring a skunk to work?

A: He wanted odor in the court.

Q: What kind of beds do mermaids sleep in?

A: Waterbeds, of course!

Q: Why did you give your dad two bananas?

A: He asked for a pair of slippers.

Q: What do you get when you cross an elephant and a kangaroo?

A: Huge holes in the ground all over Australia.

Q: How do you know elephants love swimming?

A: They always have their trunks.

Q: What do you call a mummy eating a cookie?

A: A crummy mummy.

Q: What do you do when you see a spaceman?

A: You park in it, dude.

Q: What do you call a crushed potato?

A: Squash.

Q: What do you call a train full of bubble gum?

A: A chew-chew train.

Q: What do you get when you eat caterpillars?

A: Butterflies in your stomach.

Sometimes at the top of a hill, I tuck my knees up tight to my chest and lean forward.

Really? Why?

That's just how I roll.

· ·

I returned the rest of my birdseed.

Really? Why?

Because I planted a bunch of it, and not a single bird grew.

Q: What do you call an ant sticking out of
the ground?

A: A plANT.

Q: What do you get when you cross a four-leaf
clover with poison ivy?

A: A rash of good luck.

Q: What do you call a really old ant?

A: An ANTique.

Q: What do you call a superhero that has lost all
her powers?

A: A super-ZERO.

Q: What do you do when you see an alien?

A: You give it some space.

Q: Why did the astronaut spend all her time on the back deck?

A: She preferred outer space.

Q: Why did the farmer try to get his lamb onto a rocket?

A: He'd always wanted a space-SHEEP.

Q: What happens when you smash two triangles together?

A: You get a bunch of WRECKED-angles.

Q: What do you do with elements when they're used up?

A: Barium.

Q: Why should you never eat Christmas decorations?

A: You can get tinselitis.

Q: What do you call an Easter egg from another planet?

A: An EGGS-traterrestrial.

Q: What do you call a rabbit stuck in a beehive?

A: You call it a honey bunny.

Q: What do you call a rabbit with the sniffles?

A: You call it a runny bunny.

Q: What do you call a rabbit that memorizes this joke book?

A: You call it a funny bunny.

Q: Who brings Easter eggs to the fish?

A: The oyster bunny.

Q: What is a good thing to wear at Thanksgiving?

A: A harVEST.

Q: What do you give a pet bird when it is sick?

A: Special TWEET-ment.

Q: Why did the bird leave?

A: It didn't like the way it was being tweeted.

Q: How do you know when there's an elephant hiding in your fridge?

A: There are footprints in the Jell-O.

Q: Why do elephants paint their toes different colors?

A: So they can hide in a bowl of candy.

Q: How do you get rid of ants?

A: Tell them to go find uncles.

Q: What do you say when your mom's sisters dress up in your clothes?

A: I have aunts in my pants!

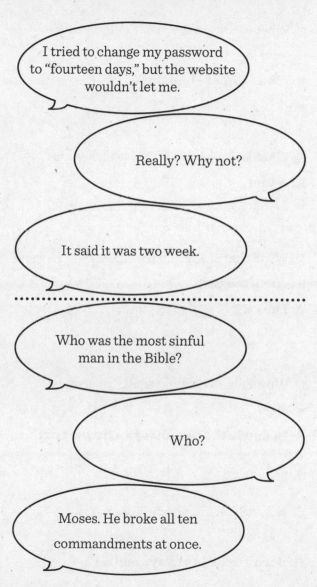

I tried to change my password to "fourteen days," but the website wouldn't let me.

Really? Why not?

It said it was two week.

Who was the most sinful man in the Bible?

Who?

Moses. He broke all ten commandments at once.

21

Q: What is gray on the inside but yellow on the outside?

A: A bus full of elephants.

Q: What is a nose that is twelve inches long?

A: A foot.

Q: What kind of vegetable would pirates never let on their boat?

A: Leeks.

Q: Why do leprechauns regularly borrow money?

A: Because they're always a little short.

Q: How do you know Lebron James is always sad?

A: Because he is always balling.

Q: Why did the farmer capture the baby deer?

A: He needed a little doe.

Q: Why did the Irish man iron his four-leaf clover?

A: He decided to press his luck.

Q: Why is it a bad idea to take a turkey to church?

A: It always uses fowl language.

Q: Why don't the lions eat the clowns?

A: The clowns taste funny.

Q: Why don't the crab and the lobster share the ocean well?

A: Because they're both really shellfish.

Q: Why don't they serve greasy food in prison?

A: Because it makes the prisoners break out.

Q: How do mountains stay warm in winter?

A: They wear their snow caps.

Q: Why did all the seals leave the United Kingdom?

A: They were afraid of Wales.

Q: Why can you eat a lot of wind?

A: Because it blows straight through you.

Q: Why can't the turkey eat a lot at Thanksgiving?

A: It is usually stuffed.

Q: Why are dalmatians terrible at hide-and-seek?

A: They're usually spotted.

Q: Why don't elephants work on computers?

A: They're afraid of the mouse.

Q: Why did the grapefruit quit the marathon?

A: It ran out of juice.

Q: Why was the fruit bowl good at poker?

A: It had a lot of pears.

Q: How is the forest like a yappie dog?

A: Both have lots of bark.

Q: Why is it dangerous to tell a duck jokes?

A: It might quack up.

Q: What happened when Moses saw the
golden calf Aaron had made?

A: He had a cow.

Q: Why is Pinocchio good at trivia questions?

A: He just nose.

Q: Why don't you ask a duck for a quarter?

A: They only have bills.

Q: Why don't fish play tennis?

A: They're afraid of the net.

Q: Why do fish have trouble going to college?

A: Because all their work is below C level.

Q: Why don't mummies meditate?

A: Because it is bad for them to unwind.

Q: What do your left foot and a bad answer have in common?

A: Neither one is right.

Q: What do cows use in math class?

A: COW-culators.

Q: How do you know leap year calendars are nicer than other years?

A: They get more dates.

Q: Why do bats get fired?

A: They're always just hanging out.

29

Q: Why are pancakes so much like baseball?

A: Both know the batter is crucial.

Q: What is the best drink for a boxer?

A: Fruit punch!

Q: What nursery rhyme does every kitten love?

A: Three Blind Mice.

Q: What subject did the kittens do well in at school?

A: MEOW-sic class.

Q: How do kittens shop?

A: From CATalogs.

Q: What do you call a bunch of fish in perfect harmony?

A: Coral singers.

Q: Why did the gardener's cake taste awful?

A: He used too much flower.

Q: What is a golfer's favorite type of music?

A: Swing.

Q: How do you make a scary fruit salad?

A: With BOO-berries.

Q: How do you improve a scary fruit dessert?

A: With I scream.

Q: What do librarians do when they want to catch smart fish?

A: They use bookworms.

Q: Why did the Irish girl move to the United States and go to bed?

A: She wanted to be an American idle.

Q: How did the math teacher fix the calculator?

A: With multiPLIERS.

Q: What kind of music did the kangaroos dance to?

A: Hip-hop.

Q: What fruit is good for scarecrows?

A: STRAW-berries.

Q: Why did the spider ace the computer test?

A: She was great on the web.

Q: Why did the tornadoes love the dance?

A: They were just twistin' the night away.

Q: How did the alien keep his pants up?

A: With his asteroid belt.

Q: Why was the mother planet so happy?

A: She got to see her sun every day.

Q: When is a good time for parents to visit an all-male boarding school?

A: On Son Day.

Q: How do scientists know the sun is happy?

A: Because they can tell it is over the moon.

Q: What was the ice cream's favorite part of church?

A: Sundae school.

Q: What song is it right to sing every morning?

A: Here comes the sun.

Q: What is the most amazing thing about Mr. and Mrs. Bigger's baby girl?

A: She's a little bigger!

Q: Why don't we know who should clean the ark?

A: It's hard to Noah!

Q: Where do you find the most cows in outer space?

A: On the moooon.

Q: What is the best music for eating nachos?

A: Guac & roll, of course!

Q: What is the English beetle's favorite sport?

A: Cricket.

Q: What is really heavy, has a lot of wheels, and flies?

A: A big garbage truck.

Q: What has six hands and six feet and loves catching flies?

A: The outfield.

Q: Where did they sign the Declaration of Independence?

A: At the bottom.

Q: Why did the kids all jump on the trampoline in winter?

A: They wanted it to be springtime.

Q: Why do bananas buy so much suntan lotion?

A: Because they peel easily!

Q: How do rock stars stay so cool?

A: They have a lot of fans.

Q: Why is basketball the messiest sport?

A: The players are always dribbling.

Q: How do you cool down a bear's cave
in summer?

A: With a bear conditioner.

Q: How do you fix a bee's hair?

A: With its honeycomb.

Q: Why can doctors wait so long?

A: They have plenty of patients.

Q: How do pilots eat their hot dogs?

A: Plane.

Q: What is the best way to get bees to school?

A: A school buzz.

Q: What can be bigger than a building but weigh nothing?

A: Its shadow.

Q: What does the buck say when its wife asks for something?

A: **Yes, deer.**

Q: What is black and white and red all over?

A: **A sunburned penguin.**

Q: What is black and white and red all over?

A: **An embarrassed zebra.**

Q: What is black and white and red all over?

A: **A skunk in a tomato fight.**

Q: What is black and white and red all over?

A: A newspaper.

Q: Why did the boat go to the store?

A: For the sail.

Q: What do you call it when people try to beat each other at running?

A: The human race.

Q: Why did cowboys ride horses?

A: They couldn't carry them.

Q: Why did the farmer put a bell on her cow?

A: Its horn didn't work.

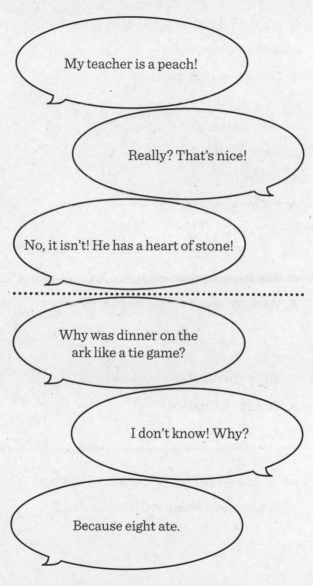

41

Q: What do you need if you have bacon and tomato on a sandwich?

A: Lettuce think about it!

Q: What did the Italian volcanoes say to each other?

A: I-a lava you-a.

Q: What did the two walls say to each other?

A: Want to meet at the corner?

Q: What did the sink say to the toilet?

A: You look flushed!

Q: What did the boat say to the paddles?

A: How about some ROW-mancing?

Q: What did one DNA say to the other?

A: Do these genes fit?

Q: What did the two strings say to each other in mid-February?

A: Happy Valen-TWINE.

Q: What did one elevator say to the other?

A: Why so down?

Q: What did one elevator say to the other?

A: What's up?

Q: Why was the toilet good at poker?

A: It always had a flush.

Q: What did the earthquake say to its parents?

A: It's not my fault!

Q: What did the spaghetti say to the linguini?

A: Penne for your thoughts?

Q: What did the buffalo say to his kid as he left for college?

A: Bison!

Q: What did the tie say to the hat?

A: You go on a head, and I'll just hang around.

Q: What did the ocean say to the beach?

A: Nothing. It waved.

Q: What do clams call a party?

A: A SHELL-abration.

Q: What do music teachers say when kids want to sing?

A: Of chorus!

Q: What did the two eyes say to each other?

A: Something smells around here.

Q: What did the doctor say to the man with a carrot in his ear?

A: I'm concerned about the way you've been eating.

Q: When are dartboards most happy?

A: When something hits the right spot.

Q: What did the marble counter say?

A: Don't take me for granite.

Q: What goes with baby corn and momma corn?

A: POPcorn.

Q: What did the nose say to the finger?

A: Please stop picking on me.

Q: What do old flowers say to new flowers?

A: Hi, bud!

Q: What did the beach say when the ocean asked him out?

A: Shore!

Q: Why not toss the margarine?

A: I'd rather see butter fly.

Q: What did the egg say to the baker?

A: You're cracking me up.

Q: What did the cat say to its baby?

A: Are you kitten me?

Q: Who do zombies run to when they are hurt?

A: Their mummies.

Q: What is a snowman's favorite cereal?

A: Frosted Flakes.

Q: Why did the art teacher tell the student to redo her painting of cattle?

A: She wanted it seen and not herd.

Q: What did the sticker say to the page?

A: I'm stuck on you.

Q: What did the fork say to the magnet?

A: WOW! You're attractive!

Q: What did the baker say to her husband?

A: I'm doughNUTS about you!

Q: Why did the pickle feel proud?

A: It was a pretty big dill.

Q: How do pigs celebrate Valentine's Day?

A: With hogs and kisses.

Q: What did the daughter owl say to her mom as she left for college?

A: Don't cry! Owl be back.

Q: What did the math teacher say to her sweetheart?

A: How much do I love thee? Let me count the ways.

Q: Why was the spoon impressed by the knife?

A: The knife was so sharp.

Q: Why was the triangle not impressed by the circle?

A: It couldn't see its point.

Q: What did the banana say to the orange about the mushroom?

A: That is a fungi!

Q: What did the hamburger call his daughter?

A: Patty.

Q: How does a teacher go swimming?

A: First, he tests the water . . .

Q: What makes a horse feel lousy in spring?

A: Hay fever.

Q: What did the paper say to the pen?

A: Write on!

Q: What did the duck say to the comedian?

A: You really quack me up!

Q: What did the psychiatrist say to the duck?

A: I think you're quackers!

Q: What did the cow say to the horse?

A: Hey man, why the long face?

Q: What did the student say when she tied her friend's laces together?

A: Have a nice trip! See you next fall!

Q: What did the beach say to the ocean?

A: Water you doing here?

Q: What did the grape do when the farmer stepped on it?

A: Not much—he just let out a little wine.

Q: What did the ground say to the earthquake?

A: Stop it! You're cracking me up!

Q: What did the hiker say at the edge of the mountain?

A: Hi, Cliff!

Q: What did the cash register say to the penny?

A: You make perfect cents.

Q: What did the judge ask the dentist?

A: Do you swear to tell the tooth, the whole tooth, and nothing but the tooth?

Q: Why were the firecrackers arguing?

A: They didn't know whose pop was bigger.

Q: Why were the firecrackers happy?

A: They had a banging good time.

Q: How do you know when the pencil sharpener has figured things out?

A: When it stops going in circles, you know it is about to get to the point.

Q: What did the lamp say when it was turned off?

A: Wow, I'm delighted.

Q: What did Tennessee?

A: Probably whatever Arkansas.

Q: What is a good snack for a toad?

A: French flies and a diet croak.

Q: What did the lettuce say before becoming a salad?

A: Go away, please. I'm not dressed yet.

Q: Why do you put the baby carrots in the vegetable drawer?

A: So they don't see the salad dressing.

Q: How is a baker like a rich woman?

A: They both have a lot of dough.

Q: What did the stoplight say to the car?

A: You should go away. I'm changing.

Q: Why did the basketball player throw away his passport?

A: His coach yelled at him to stop traveling.

Q: What did the two lightning bugs say to each other?

A: You glow, girl!

Q: What did the doctor say to the rocketship right before it left for space?

A: Be sure to get your booster shot!

Q: What did the kitten say when it fell?

A: MeOW!

Q: What did the doctor give the sick kitten?

A: A PURR-scription.

Q: How did the optometrist help the spider's business?

A: She greatly improved the spider's web sight.

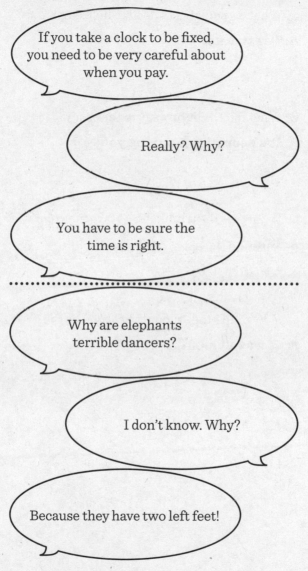

If you take a clock to be fixed, you need to be very careful about when you pay.

Really? Why?

You have to be sure the time is right.

Why are elephants terrible dancers?

I don't know. Why?

Because they have two left feet!

Q: What do podiatrists need to help elephants?

A: Toe trucks.

Q: What did the bunny say to the carrot?

A: It's been nice gnawing you!

Q: What was the trumpeters's favorite color?

A: Blew.

Q: Why didn't the students hear the music?

A: It wasn't aloud.

Q: What do bakers put on their beds?

A: Cookie sheets.

Q: What did the burrito say to the nacho?

A: Where you bean?

Q: What snacks can you make right on
the beach?

A: Sandwiches.

Q: What did the toast say to the knife?

A: Stop buttering me up.

Q: What did the outfielder say to the baseball?

A: Catch you later!

Q: What did the teacher say to the unruly bees?

A: Please start BEE-having.

Q: What did the bee say when she returned from work?

A: Honey, I'm home!

Q: What did the lawyer say when the judge called for order?

A: I don't know. Maybe a chicken sandwich and fries.

Q: What did the chemist say to the atom that thought it lost an electron?

A: Are you positive?

Q: Why do you never ask a golfer the time?

A: Because they always say FORE!

Q: What is the worst kind of flower to give on Valentine's Day?

A: Cauliflower.

Q: Why is 4+4 never hungry?

A: Because it already eight.

Q: What is the best thing to feed a snowman?

A: Chilly.

Q: What did the tree say to the ornament?

A: How long are you hanging around?

Q: What do eggs do when you read them this book?

A: They crack up.

Q: What should you serve a skeleton with its coffee?

A: A mop.

Q: Where do scary monsters win crowns?

A: At BOO-ty pageants.

Q: What did the bat say to the pretty girl?

A: Mind if I hang around?

Q: What did the light bulb say to the pretty girl?

A: I love you watts and watts.

Q: What did the two Velcro pieces say to each other?

A: We've really gotta stick together.

Q: What did the dolphin do when she got angry?

A: She flipped out.

Q: If you have three dozen hamburgers and you eat half of them, what do you have?

A: A stomachache.

Q: Where do penguins keep their money?

A: In snowbanks.

Q: How does a duck detective catch a bad guy?

A: He quacks the case.

Q: What did the queen name the knight who discovered the wheel?

A: Sir Cumference.

Q: What is something you almost never eat right before bedtime?

A: Breakfast.

Q: What is something you never eat for dinner?

A: Lunch.

Q: Why did the turkey get cut from his baseball team?

A: Too many fowl balls.

Q: Name ten things you can always count on.

A: Your fingers.

Q: Why is the ocean stronger than the beach?

A: The ocean has more mussels.

Q: What tree might grow fingers?

A: A palm.

Q: Why were the dark ages so dark?

A: Because of all the knights.

Q: What is really easy to get into but really hard to get out of?

A: Trouble.

Q: Why were the fish upset with the electric eels?

A: The eels' behavior was shocking.

Q: What is the best-smelling thing at the dinner table?

A: Probably your nose.

Q: What did Adam call the first 365 days after God gave him Eve?

A: New Eve's Year.

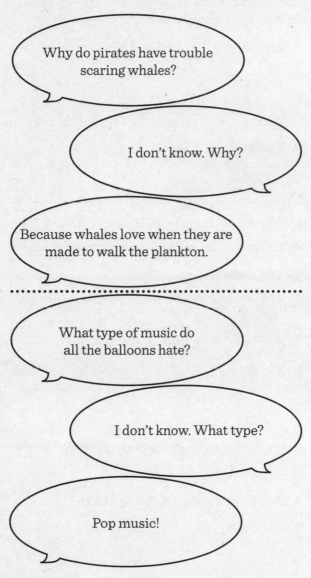

Why do pirates have trouble scaring whales?

I don't know. Why?

Because whales love when they are made to walk the plankton.

What type of music do all the balloons hate?

I don't know. What type?

Pop music!

Q: Why is England so wet?

A: The queen has reigned over it for ages.

Q: What country probably has the most fish?

A: Finland.

Q: Why do dolphins make so few mistakes?

A: Because almost everything they do is on porpoise.

Q: What dies without living?

A: Batteries.

Q: When is a good time to look for money outside?

A: Anytime there's a change in the weather.

Q: What is Frosty's favorite time of the school day?

A: Snow-and-tell.

Q: How do you give a dolphin directions?

A: However you like, but be sure you're very Pacific.

Q: How do you know it's going to start raining candy?

A: It starts with little sprinkles.

Q: What does a skeleton order for dinner?

A: Lots of ribs.

Q: What do teddy bears sit on?

A: FURniture.

Q: What do sharks like on their peanut butter sandwich?

A: Lots of jellyfish.

Q: Do you know when you SHOULD put a cart before a horse?

A: When you are making a dictionary.

Q: What did my watch do when dinner didn't fill it up?

A: It went back four seconds.

Q: How is KFC like a marching band?

A: Both have a lot of drumsticks.

Q: What did triceratops sit on?

A: Their tricera-BOTTOMS, I think.

Q: Why did the cow stop singing?

A: Because it was really horse.

Q: What is the invisible man's favorite drink?

A: Evaporated milk.

Q: What do evil chickens lay?

A: Deviled eggs.

Q: Why do oranges score so high on tests?

A: They concentrate.

Q: How does the sun get around?

A: It SOLARblades.

Q: How do you start a reindeer race?

A: You say, "Ready, set, HO! HO! HO!"

Q: What does a kitten do in the rain?

A: It gets wet.

Q: What are the best shoes for spies to wear?

A: Sneakers.

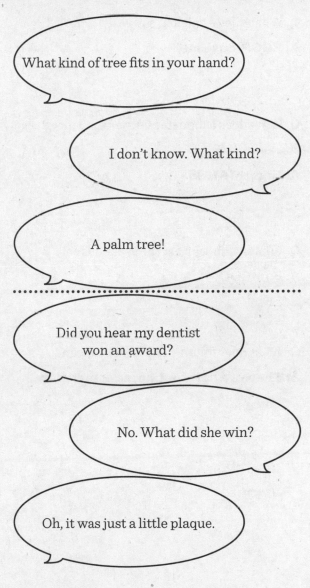

73

Q: What does a chicken say when it burps?

A: EGGS-cuse me.

Q: What does a monster farmer keep in its stables?

A: NightMARES.

Q: What is the scariest thing pandas eat?

A: BamBOO!

Q: What does finding a horseshoe mean?

A: There's a barefoot horse somewhere.

Q: When is Christmas before Independence Day?

A: In the dictionary.

Q: What did one color say to the other?

A: Please don't use that tone with me!

Q: What does the Statue of Liberty stand for?

A: It has no choice—it can't sit down.

Q: What goes up when the rain falls down?

A: An umbrella.

Q: What question can you ask that will almost always be answered YES?

A: What does Y-E-S spell?

Q: What is the wettest letter in the alphabet?

A: C.

Q: Athletes get athlete's foot, but what do astronauts get?

A: Missile toe.

Q: Why do some machines hum?

A: Because they don't know the words.

Q: What dog is great at keeping time?

A: A watch dog.

Q: What do you use to clean a puppy?

A: Sham-POODLE.

Q: How do you light up a soccer stadium?

A: With a soccer match.

Q: Why is bubble gum bad at math tests?

A: It keeps getting stuck on the problems.

Q: What is big and green and fuzzy and if it fell from the roof, it could kill you?

A: A pool table.

Q: What does a pirate charge for piercings?

A: About a buck an ear.

Q: What does a chimney cost?

A: Nothing at all. It's on the house.

Q: Why is a football game worth a dollar?

A: Because it has four quarters.

Q: Why was the golfer kicked out of the coffee shop?

A: He kept putting his golf ball on the tea.

Q: If you have three basketballs in one hand and four footballs in the other hand, what do you have?

A: HUGE hands.

Q: What school do all the graduates drop out of?

A: Skydiving school.

Q: What is the real key to a great Thanksgiving dinner?

A: A TurKEY.

Q: Why do chickens lay eggs?

A: Because if they dropped them, they would break.

Q: Where do all the planets and the stars go to school?

A: At the UNIVERSE-ity.

Q: Why were the scrambled eggs cut from the track team?

A: They kept getting beat.

Q: What did the four fingers say to the thumb as they warmed up?

A: Isn't it great to be in glove with each other?

Q: Why did the music teacher have trouble starting her car?

A: She'd left all her keys in the piano.

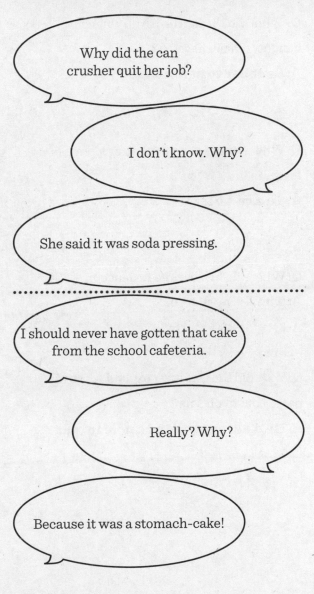

Q: What did the hairbrush do when her daughter misbehaved?

A: Sent her to her broom.

Q: Where did the parrot go after losing its feathers?

A: To a re-tailer.

Q: Where do Frisbees go to dance?

A: The flying disc-o.

Q: Why did the golfer get excited when his pants caught on a nail?

A: He'd always wanted a hole in one.

Q: What's every cow's favorite city?

A: Mooooo York City.

Q: What is every cow's favorite heavenly body?

A: The moooooon.

Q: What did the sheep say to the Terminator?

A: I'll be baaaaaaack.

Q: Where do all the sheep go on vacation?

A: The Baaaaahamas.

Q: What did the chef give his wife for
Valentine's Day?

A: A hug and a quiche.

Q: What did the dog say when his friend failed obedience school?

A: Man, that's ruffffff.

Q: What is every dog's favorite movie?

A: *The Woof of Wall Street*.

Q: Why did the detective finally leave the dog alone?

A: He realized he'd been barking up the wrong tree.

Q: Which side of a duck has the most feathers?

A: The outside.

Q: What flies around the library every night?

A: Alpha bats.

Q: What is a terrible pillar to use when building tall buildings?

A: A caterpillar.

Q: What animal is at EVERY baseball game?

A: The bat.

Q: A cat might have nine lives, but which animal has more?

A: The toad. It croaks every night.

Q: What does a dog do that a human steps into?

A: Pants.

Q: Which animal needs oil?

A: The mouse. It squeaks all the time.

Q: What key is terrible at unlocking doors?

A: The monKEY.

Q: What kind of stories do giraffes tell?

A: Tall tales.

Q: What flits and flies as it is born, lies while it is resting, then runs when it is finished?

A: Snow.

Q: How do you know it is cold at Christmas?

A: Because it is Decembrrrrr.

Q: Why is it impossible to fool a snake?

A: You can't pull its leg.

Q: How do you know the snowman is freaking out?

A: You see it melt down.

Q: Is chicken for dinner good for you?

A: Not if you're the chicken!

Q: What kind of water never freezes?

A: Hot water.

Q: What's a frog's favorite sport?

A: CROAK-uet.

Q: What is a frog's favorite drink?

A: CROAK-a-Cola.

Q: What is the frog's favorite pie?

A: CROAK-onut cream.

Q: What is a frog's favorite forest friend?

A: The ribbit.

Q: Why was the skunk crying at the movie?

A: It was really SCENT-amental.

Q: What did the pickle say when his friend
got upset?

A: Man, just dill with it.

Q: If April showers bring May flowers, what do
May flowers bring?

A: Pilgrims.

Q: How is the moon held together?

A: **With moon beams.**

Q: Why are bikes the laziest thing in the garage?

A: **They are always two tired.**

Q: Why couldn't the captain ever play cards?

A: **Because he was always on the deck.**

Q: Why couldn't the runner listen to her music?

A: **She had broken the record.**

Q: Why couldn't the owl use the computer?

A: **He'd just eaten the mouse.**

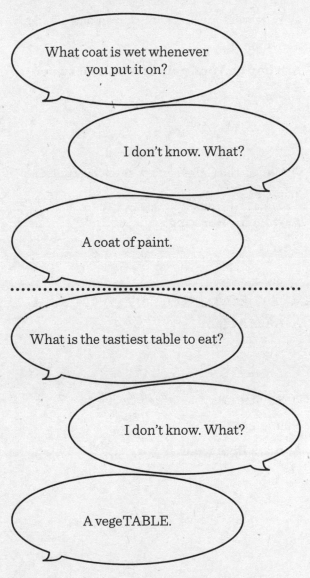

Q: Why were the elephants too embarrassed to go swimming?

A: They had one pair of trunks between them.

Q: Why is the Canadian goose such a rude driver?

A: It keeps honking.

Q: Who is every bee's favorite astronaut?

A: Buzz Aldrin.

Q: What is every bee's favorite movie character?

A: Buzz Lightyear.

Q: Why do bees have trouble making friends?

A: They're real busybodies.

Q: Why couldn't the skunk get elected?

A: Her platform really stunk.

Q: Why did the skunks quit four-wheeling?

A: They kept getting stunk.

Q: Why couldn't the skunk use the restroom?

A: It was out of odor.

Q: Why would none of the animals go to the skunk's party?

A: The skunk's parties always stink.

Q: What falls all the time but never gets hurt?

A: Rain.

Q: What flower is the best for kissing?

A: Tulips.

Q: What jam do you never want for breakfast?

A: A traffic jam.

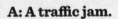

Q: What animal goes *zzub zzub*?

A: A bee flying backward.

Q: What animal goes *ffur ffur*?

A: A dog running backward.

Q: What animal goes *tooh tooh*?

A: An owl flying backward!

Q: What time is it when your tooth starts to really ache?

A: Tooth-hurty.

Q: What time is it when you win a watch in your breakfast cereal?

A: Free o'clock.

Q: What time is it right after dinner?

A: Ate.

Q: What time is it when your clock strikes thirteen?

A: Time to get a new clock.

Q: What time is it when people start throwing things at you?

A: Time to duck.

Q: Why do Canadian geese fly south?

A: The drive was getting too busy.

Q: How does a monster cook eggs?

A: It terror-FRIES them.

Q: What can spend all day in the freezer and still come out hot?

A: Jalapeños.

Q: What do you call a bossy math teacher?

A: A hard ruler.

Q: What is served regularly but often sent back?

A: A tennis ball.

Q: What can you catch easily but never throw back?

A: A cold.

Q: Why didn't the skeleton cross the road?

A: He didn't have the guts.

Q: What is the best way to send your wishes to God?

A: Use KNEE-mail.

Q: Why didn't the rope get any presents on Christmas morning?

A: It was knotty.

Q: Why did the pretzel twist?

A: It had seen the bunny hop.

Q: Why didn't the skeleton dance along?

A: It had no body to dance with.

Q: Why did the oven skip college?

A: It already had 400 degrees.

Q: Why do dimes supervise nickels?

A: Because they have more cents.

Q: Why did the archaeologist love old french fries?

A: Because they were made in ancient Greece.

Q: What do you call flying skunks?

A: SMELLY-copters.

Q: What kind of hair does the ocean have?

A: Wavy.

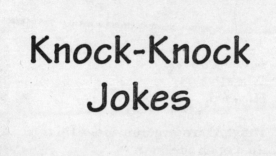

Knock-Knock Jokes

Knock knock!
Who's there?
Goliath.
Goliath who?
Goliath down, David. You look tired.

Knock knock!
Who's there?
Howard.
Howard who?
Howard are ya gonna make this? Just open the door.

Knock knock!
Who's there?
Howard.
Howard who?
Howard you feel if you were stuck out here?

Knock knock!
Who's there?
Ice cream.
Ice cream who?
**ICE CREAM AND SCREAM
UNTIL YOU OPEN THE DOOR!**

Knock knock!
Who's there?
Police.
Police who?
**Police open the door! It is cold
out here.**

Knock knock!
Who's there?
Will.
Will who?
Will you please open the door?

Knock knock!
Who's there?
Will.
Will who?
Will it make any difference what name I say?

Knock knock!
Who's there?
Will.
Will who?
Will you always remember me?

Knock knock!
Who's there?
Will.
Will who?
Will you remember me in twenty years?

Knock knock!
Who's there?
Will.
Will who?
Will you remember me in twenty days?

Knock knock!
Who's there?
Will.
Will who?
Will you remember me in twenty minutes?

Knock knock!
Who's there?
Will.
Will who?
Will you remember me in twenty seconds?

Knock knock!
Who's there?
Will.
Will who?
YOU FORGOT ME ALREADY?!?!

Knock knock!
Who's there?
Antelopes.
Antelopes who?
Antelopes so she can marry your uncle.

Knock knock!
Who's there?
A broken needle.
A broken needle who?
Aaah, never mind. It's pointless.

Knock knock!
Who's there?
A parrot.
A parrot who?
A parrot who?

Knock knock!
Who's there?
A herd.
A herd who?
A herd this is the place to be!

Knock knock!
Who's there?
A rock.
A rock who?
A rock Obama!

Knock knock!
Who's there?
Aaron.
Aaron who?
Aaron't you feeling a little silly?
You're looking right at me!

Knock knock!
Who's there?
Aaron.
Aaron who?
Aaron't you going to open the
door already?!?!?

Knock knock!
Who's there?
Abby.
Abby who?
Abby just stung my leg! Please let
me in.

Knock knock!
Who's there?
Abby.
Abby who?
Abby a friend of yours if you let me in.

Knock knock!
Who's there?
Abby.
Abby who?
Abby back. This is taking too long.

Knock knock!
Who's there?
Abe.
Abe who?
Abe E C D E F G . . .

Knock knock!
Who's there?
Beets.
Beets who?
Beets me. Now, can you please open the door?

Knock knock!
Who's there?
Ben.
Ben who?
Ben that long that you forgot who I am?

Knock knock!
Who's there?
Boo.
Boo who?
Relax! I'm just telling a joke. You don't need to start crying.

Knock knock!
Who's there?
Butter.
Butter who?
Butter open the door or I'm gonna knock again.

Knock knock!
Who's there?
Canoe.
Canoe who?
Canoe not tell by looking at me?

Knock knock!
Who's there?
Canoe.
Canoe who?
Canoe open the door? You know who it is!

Knock knock!
Who's there?
Cargo.
Cargo who?
No, silly, car go *honk honk*, or *beep beep*, or *vroom vroom*.

Knock knock!
Who's there?
Cheese.
Cheese who?
Cheese cute. Let her in.

Knock knock!
Who's there?
Claire.
Claire who?
Clairely it is me! You're looking right at me!

Knock knock!
Who's there?
Claire.
Claire who?
Claire the way! I'm coming in now.

Knock knock!
Who's there?
Claws.
Claws who?
Claws the door the minute I come in—I think I'm being followed!

Knock knock!
Who's there?
Monkey.
Monkey who?
No, owl says who. Monkey says oooh oooh, aaah aaah!

Knock knock!
Who's there?
Dish.
Dish who?
Dish is boring out here. Please let me in.

Knock knock!
Who's there?
Dish.
Dish who?
Dish can't be happening! I know you know me!

Knock knock!
Who's there?
Doris.
Doris who?
Doris locked. Can you please unlock it?

Knock knock!
Who's there?
Enno.
Enno who?
Enno way you don't know me.

Knock knock!
Who's there?
Fanny.
Fanny who?
Fanny body calls, tell them I'm out front.

Knock knock!
Who's there?
Goat.
Goat who?
Goat to the door and see for yourself.

Knock knock!
Who's there?
Harry.
Harry who?
**Harry up and answer the door!
I'm freezing.**

Knock knock!
Who's there?
Honeybee.
Honeybee who?
**Honeybee a sweetheart and open
the door.**

Knock knock!
Who's there?
Iva.
Iva who?
Iva cold. Please let me in.

Knock knock!
Who's there?
Iva.
Iva who?
Iva sore hand from all this knocking!

Knock knock!
Who's there?
Leaf.
Leaf who?
Leaf me alone! I like it out here!

Knock knock!
Who's there?
Leaf.
Leaf who?
Leaf me out here much longer and I'll leave!

Knock knock!
Who's there?
Lettuce.
Lettuce who?
**Lettuce think about it for a
minute . . . Who else could it be?**

Knock knock!
Who's there?
Mary.
Mary who?
**Mary me! I would make a great
partner.**

Knock knock!
Who's there?
Mary and Abby.
Mary and Abby who?
**Mary Christmas and Abby
New Year!**

Knock knock!
Who's there?
Nana.
Nana who?
Nana your business. Just open this door!

Knock knock!
Who's there?
Nana.
Nana who?
Nana, Nana. Nana, Nana! Hey, hey, hey! Goodbye!

Knock knock!
Who's there?
Noah.
Noah who?
Noah guy who might open this door?

Knock knock!
Who's there?
Noah.
Noah who?
Noah way-a I'm-a gonna tell ya!

Knock knock!
Who's there?
Olive.
Olive who?
Olive right next door. You don't know me?

Knock knock!
Who's there?
Olive.
Olive who?
Olive you. Now give me a hug.

Knock knock!
Who's there?
Just a little girl.
Just a little girl who?
Just a little girl who wants to say hi!

Knock knock!
Who's there?
Pecan.
Pecan who?
Pecan someone else. I just want in.

Knock knock!
Who's there?
Phillip.
Phillip who?
Phillip my cup. I'm thirsty.

Knock knock!
Who's there?
Snow.
Snow who?
Snow use trying to be friends if you can't remember my name.

Knock knock!
Who's there?
Tennis.
Tennis who?
Tennis more than enough jokes for now.

Knock knock!
Who's there?
Theodore.
Theodore who?
Theodore is locked. Can you please open it?

Knock knock!
Who's there?
Theo.
Theo who?
Theo comes after the *n* and before the *p*.

Knock knock!
Who's there?
Tyrone.
Tyrone who?
Tyrone shoes. I'm not gonna do it.

Knock knock!
Who's there?
Yukon.
Yukon who?
Yukon answer the door anytime you're ready.

Knock knock!
Who's there?
Yukon.
Yukon who?
Yukon let me in, or Yukon keep the door closed. It is up to you!

Knock knock!
Who's there?
Ken.
Ken who?
Ken you not tell by the sound of my voice?

Knock knock!
Who's there?
Zain.
Zain who?
Zaint no way this isn't your favorite joke book!